What Color Is Your Skin?

Written by Lisa M. Reed

Illustrated by Iwan Darmawan

Text and Illustration Copyright © 2019, 2017 by Lisa M. Reed

All rights reserved.
No part of this book may be reproduced or transmitted in any form
or by any means, electronic or mechanical, including photocopying, recording,
or by any information storage or retrieval system, without permission in writing
by the author.

Published in the United States
3rd Printing September 2019
Library of Congress Cataloging-in Publication Data
Reed, Lisa M., 2010
What Color is Your Skin? / by Lisa M. Reed-Third Edition.
www.whatcolorisyourskin.com

ISBN 978-1-727-31285-0 (paperback)

Printed in the US

Illustrated by Iwan Darmawan

Book design by Bluebobo

Summary: Arianna asks why her skin color is not the same color as
her grandma's. She learns that children come in many colors.

Acknowledgements

Thank you to my granddaughter, Arianna, who at the age of four gave me a way to answer a very tough question.

Thank you to every person that helped me on my journey to complete this book.

A very special thank you to the Kaushal and the Odom families who helped get me through my writer's block and make this dream real.

A final thanks to Cyndie Beacham, Toni Carter, Morgan Pettus and Arvi Kaushal who became my unofficial editors.

"What Color Is Your Skin" is a creative approach to teaching our youth to value the differences that we all have while loving themselves and being comfortable with how God created them. This book dares to explore the oftentimes taboo issues of diversity and various skin tones that are ever present in our society. This story innocently addresses a conversation that needs to be awakened within all of us starting at a child's level. Sharing this story with our children will allow us to learn to appreciate the diversity and cultural differences that we all bring to the table.

Children will enjoy the comparison of the many ice cream flavors to the various skin colors. As ice cream has more than just one delicious flavor that tastes great, we have many skin colors and there is not only one that is best.

The book has the underlying theme that teaches children that "we are all great!" Ms. Reed does an exceptional job tackling such a sensitive issue that needs to be in the forefront of the learning perspective. Children can learn to love one another just as they love the wide varieties of their favorite treat - ice cream! I will be sharing this story with my 4th graders this school year as well as my own beautiful "coffee brown" children!

TyRonda Mott TyRonda Mott, MBA
4th Grade English Language Arts Teacher
Spring Independent School District

'What Color Is Your Skin?' is a wonderful children's book that I found to be light-spirited and educational. Actually, I believe that adults can benefit from the story also as it serves to remind us of the beautiful diversity of humanity that should be celebrated. This is such a nice, inspirational story that can be a positive tool to bring children together with happiness and joy in their curiosity.

I truly enjoyed reading this book and recommend it to be widely read and available in schools especially.

Cyd Webster Beacham Author,
Struck By Lightning and HB

Arianna is very excited about going to her grandma's house for a visit.

She grabs her bag and hops into her mother's car, happy to go!

"Are you ready for a visit with Grandma? Asks her mother. "Oh yes!" answers Arianna. "Let's go!"

At last, they arrive and Grandma is waiting with open arms.

"Goodbye Mom, goodbye little brother, I'll see you later", she yells as she waves goodbye.

Grandma asks, "What would you like to do today?"

"Can we go get ice cream?"
"Of course dear", replies her grandma.

When they arrive at the ice cream shop, grandma helps Arianna out of the car.

As her grandma reaches for her hand, Arianna sees her skin is not same as her grandma's.

"Grandma, my mommy's skin is white and my daddy's skin is brown.

My skin is like mommy's. What color is your skin?"

Her grandma looks at her lovingly and says,
"God made people in many different colors."

"There are many flavors of ice cream,
just like there are many different colors
of children all around the world."

Arianna is amazed at all the colors of ice cream. "Wow!" says Arianna, "There are so many different ice cream colors. I don't know which one to choose!"

Her grandma says, "I'm going to choose butter pecan because that is most like the color of your daddy and I."

Arianna asks, "What color do you think I am?"
Her grandma replies, "I think you are like the color butter cream."

Arianna looks at a little boy at the first table and asks, "What color is he?"

The little boy hears Arianna talking to her grandma and replies,

"Hi, I am Jeremy from New Jersey.
I am like the color Coffee."

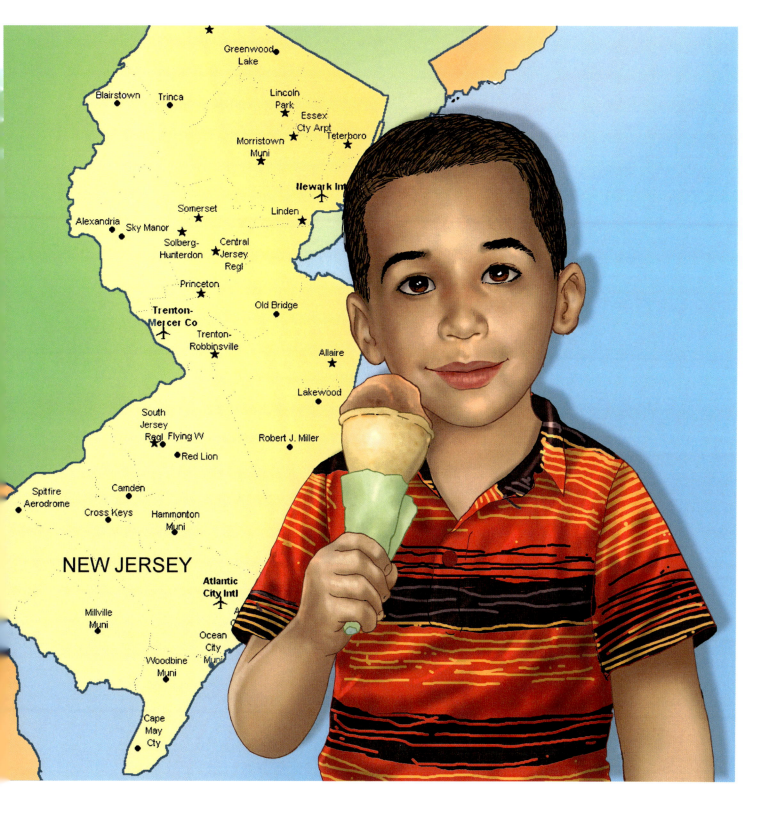

And just like a game, Widelene at the next table, hears Jeremy and says,

"Hi, I am Widelene from Haiti.
I am like the color Cacao."

Then each child chimes in because
they want to choose a color too.

"Hi, I am Guan-yin from China.
I am like the color Eggnog."

"Hi I am Isha from India.
I am like the color Butter Pecan."

"Hi, I am Saul from Puerto Rico.
I am like the color Café con Leche."

"Hi, I am Manu from the
Republic of the Congo.
I am like the color Chocolate Fudge."

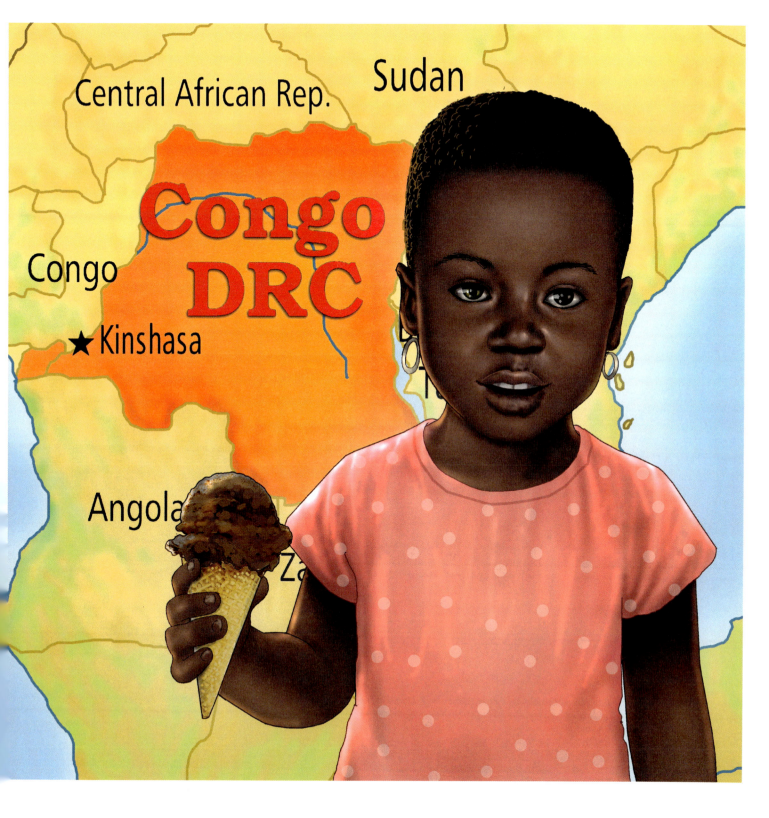

"Hi, I am Jung from South Korea.
I am like the color Almond Crunch."

"Hi, I am Pierre from France.
I am like the color Vanilla Bean."

"Hi, I am Aaliyah from Syria.
I am like the color Caramel."

"You see Arianna," her grandma says,
"God created all of us in many colors,
just like the ice cream we all love!"

Tell us who you are and create your flavor of ice cream

Hi, I am _____

from _____.

I am like the color _____.

Go to our website at **www.whatcolorisyourskin.com** to create your ice cream flavor and see other flavors created by children all over the world.

The End!

Made in the USA
Monee, IL
29 September 2021